THEORY PAPERS

Robert Pace

ASSIGNED_____ COMPLETED_____ COMMENTS:							
WEEK	M	T	W	Th	F	S	Su
1st							
2nd							
3rd							

Fill in the missing note names.

madison

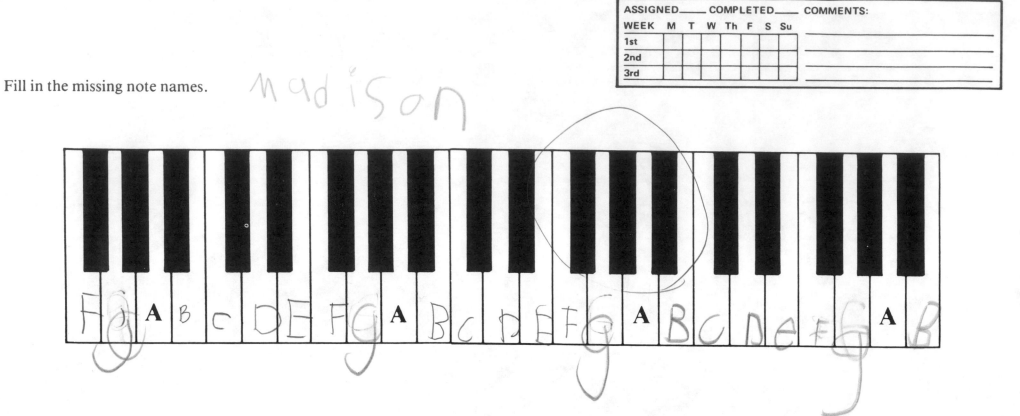

Fill in all of the note names.

D   D D D

Madison

ASSIGNED____ COMPLETED____								COMMENTS:
WEEK	M	T	W	Th	F	S	Su	
1st								
2nd								
3rd								

Print the names of the notes beginning with A.

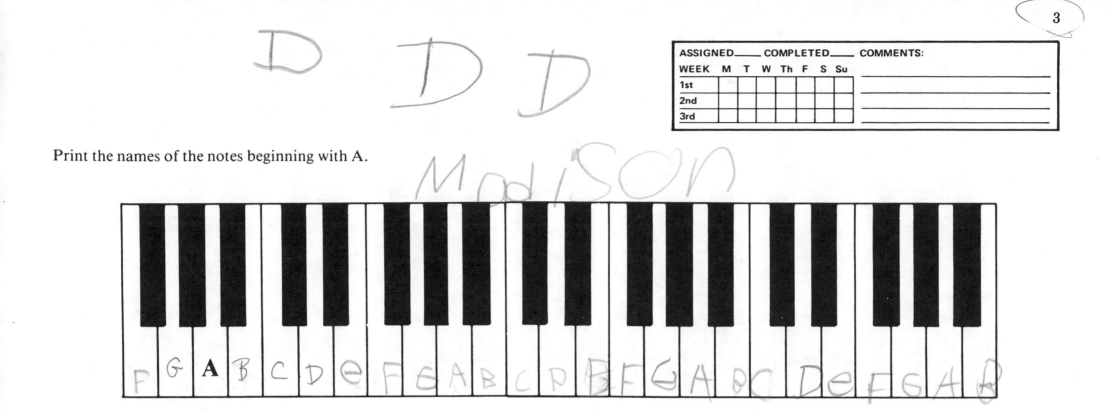

F G A B C D E F G A B C D E F G A B C D E F G A B

Now print the note names beginning with C.

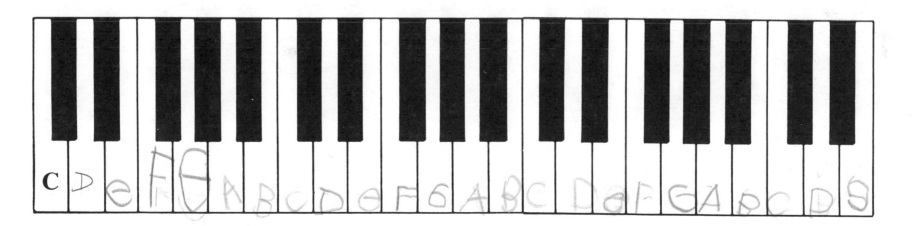

C D E F G A B C D E F G A B C D E F G A B C D E

ASSIGNED____ COMPLETED____ COMMENTS:							
WEEK	M	T	W	Th	F	S	Su
1st							
2nd							
3rd							

Print the letter names G, A, and B on all of the keys where they belong.

Print the letter names C, D, and E on this keyboard.

ASSIGNED____ COMPLETED____	COMMENTS:
WEEK M T W Th F S Su	_____
1st	_____
2nd	_____
3rd	_____

Print the letter names A, C, E, and G where they belong.

Print the letter names G, B, D, and F on this keyboard.

SKIPS AND STEPS

| ASSIGNED____ COMPLETED____ | COMMENTS: |

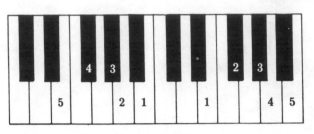

Write the fingering for both left and right hands in the blanks, then play in E Major.

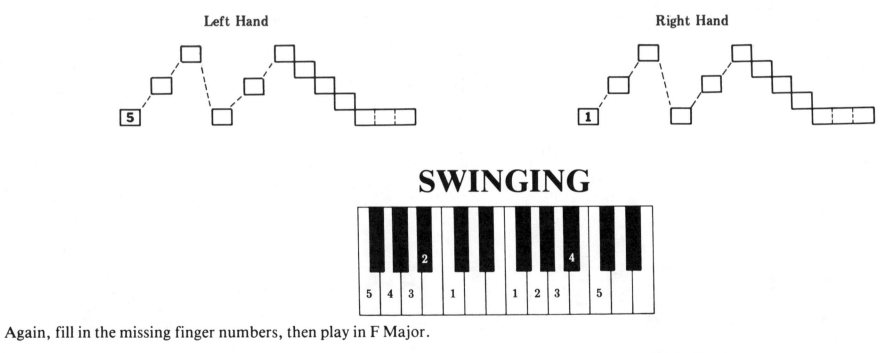

SWINGING

Again, fill in the missing finger numbers, then play in F Major.

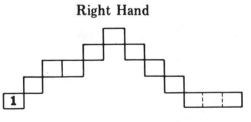

OLD WOMAN

ASSIGNED____ COMPLETED____	COMMENTS:							
WEEK	M	T	W	Th	F	S	Su	
1st								
2nd								
3rd								

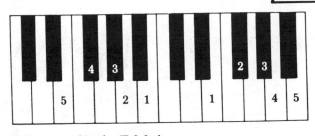

Fill in the fingering for the left hand of "Old Woman," then play in E Major.

Left Hand

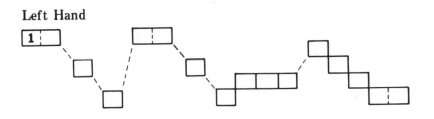

OLD MAN

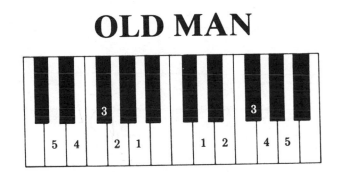

Fill in the right hand fingering for "Old Man" and play in D Major.

Right Hand

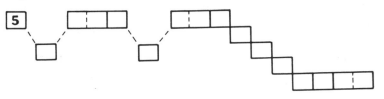

GRAND STAFF

This is the *grand staff*. Fill in the missing letter names. Find each one on your piano.

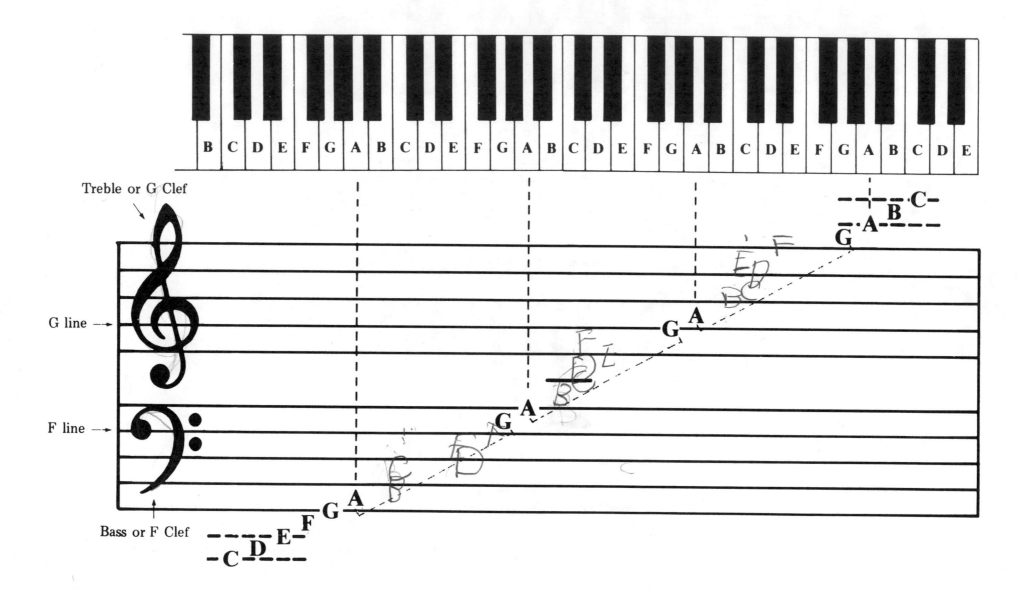

TREBLE CLEF

Play with Right hand

1st Day   Make the straight line   then make the curved line.   **2nd Day** Trace over these.   **3rd Day** Trace over these.

Draw three treble clefs each day.

4th Day   **5th Day**   **6th Day**

BASS CLEF

Play with left hand

1st Day   Make the curved line,   then place the 2 dots.   **2nd Day** Trace over these.   **3rd Day** Trace over these.

Draw three bass clefs each day.

4th Day   **5th Day**   **6th Day**

TIME SIGNATURES

Fill in the time signature.

Draw the missing bar lines.

There are seven flats in the key of C♭ Major and seven sharps in the key of C♯ Major.

ASSIGNED____ COMPLETED____ COMMENTS:							
WEEK	M	T	W	Th	F	S	Su
1st							
2nd							
3rd							

But since there is very little music written in these keys we shall spend our time now on the other six keys.

Key of G♭ Major

Trace the six ♭ signs here in treble and bass clef.

Make a ♭ sign at the end of each line.

Key of F♯ Major

Trace the six ♯ signs here in treble and bass clef.

Make a ♯ sign at the end of each line.

ASSIGNED____ COMPLETED____ COMMENTS:							
WEEK	M	T	W	Th	F	S	Su
1st							
2nd							
3rd							

Write the letter names of the lines and spaces from A to G.

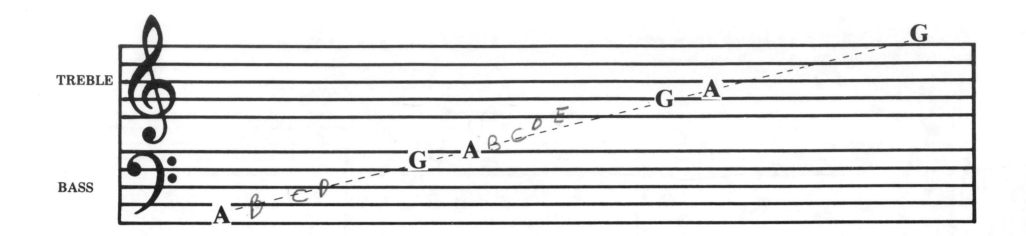

Write the letter name of each line and space.

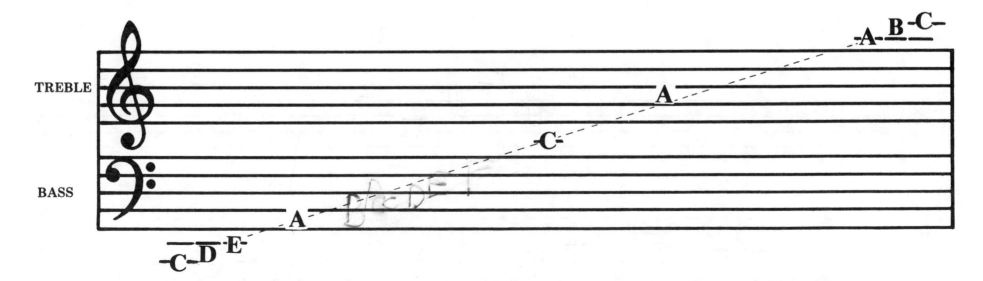

ASSIGNED____ COMPLETED____ COMMENTS:							
WEEK	M	T	W	Th	F	S	Su
1st							
2nd							
3rd							

Each day make a key signature in both treble and bass clefs.

1st Day   2nd Day   3rd Day

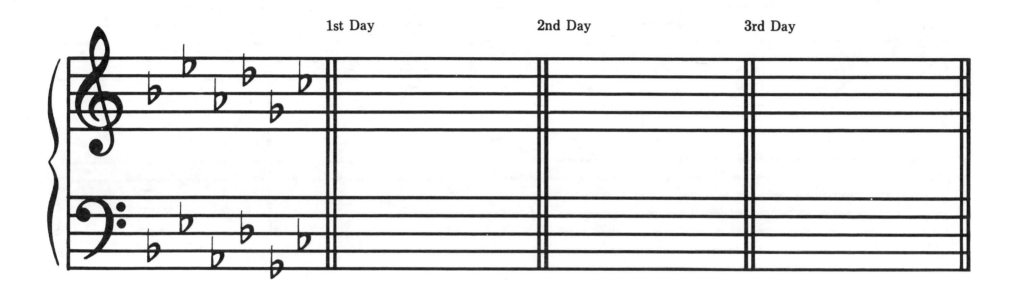

4th Day   5th Day   6th Day

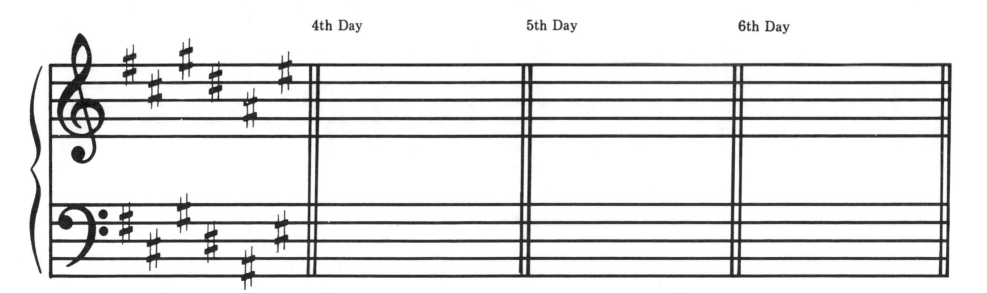

GRAND STAFF

Write the correct letter names in both treble and bass clefs.

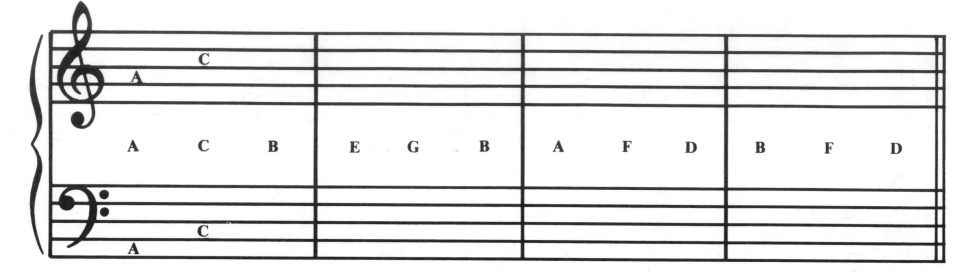

Make whole notes in treble and bass clefs for each of these letters.

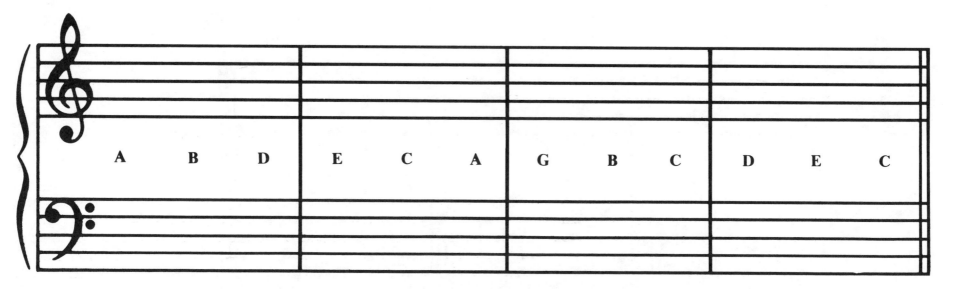

ASSIGNED____ COMPLETED____ COMMENTS:								
WEEK	M	T	W	Th	F	S	Su	
1st								
2nd								
3rd								

Make a key signature in both treble and bass clefs each day.

1st Day   2nd Day   3rd Day

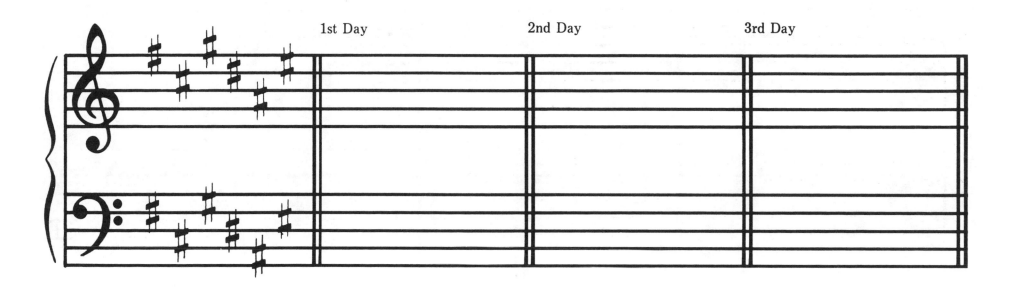

4th Day   5th Day   6th Day

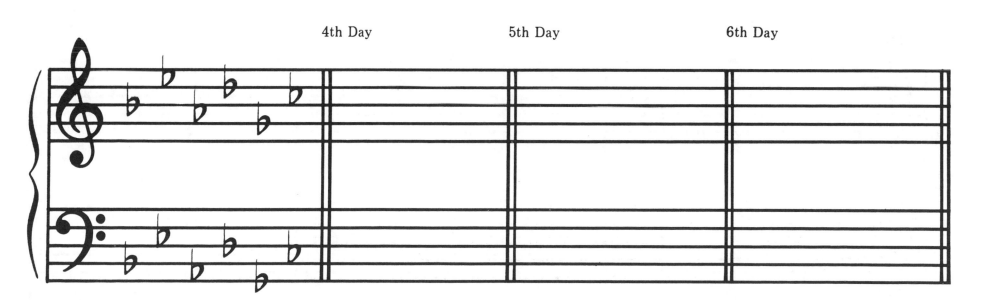

ASSIGNED____ COMPLETED____ COMMENTS:								
WEEK	M	T	W	Th	F	S	Su	
1st								
2nd								
3rd								

Make the following flat key signatures in both treble and bass clefs.
Fill in the name of each.

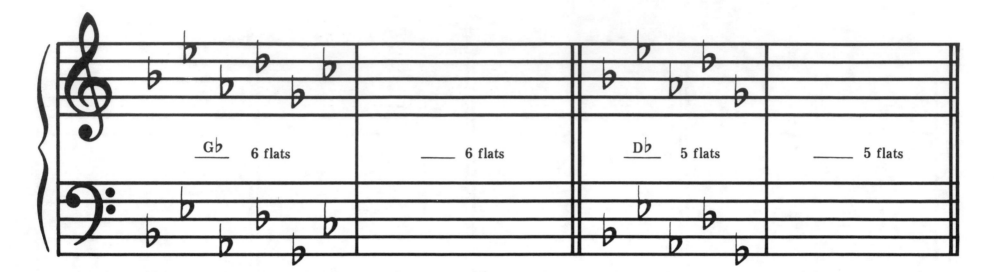

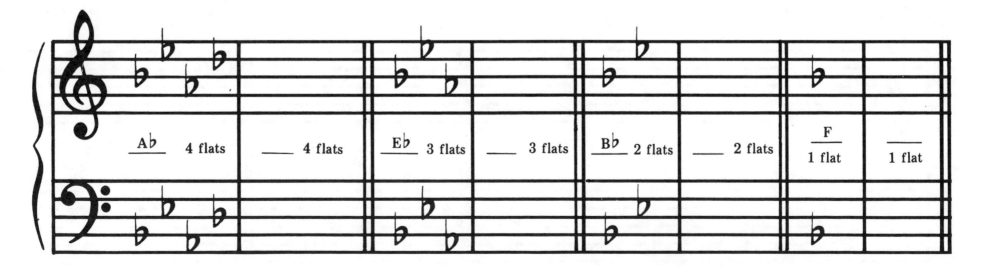

ASSIGNED____			COMPLETED____				COMMENTS:
WEEK	M	T	W	Th	F	S	Su
1st							
2nd							
3rd							

Write each of these key signatures in treble and bass clef and fill in the name.

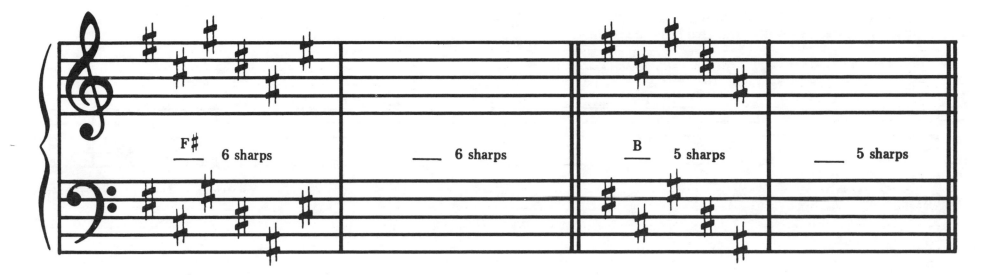

F♯ — 6 sharps   ___ 6 sharps   B — 5 sharps   ___ 5 sharps

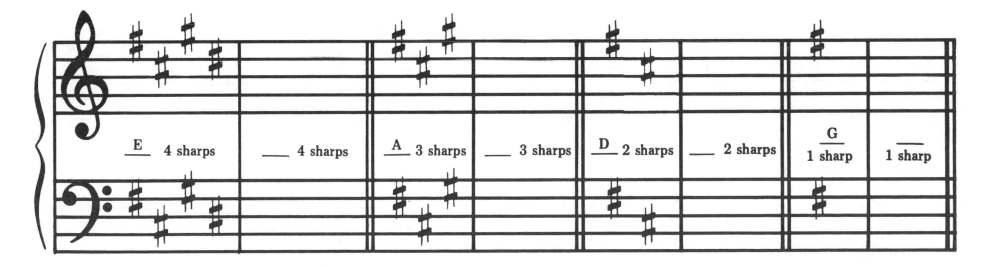

E — 4 sharps   ___ 4 sharps   A — 3 sharps   ___ 3 sharps   D — 2 sharps   ___ 2 sharps   G — 1 sharp   ___ 1 sharp

2244

ASSIGNED____ COMPLETED____ COMMENTS:							
WEEK	M	T	W	Th	F	S	Su
1st							
2nd							
3rd							

Here is a theme and variation.

Make up variations of your own by changing a note or two in the second or third measures.

After playing many variations write your two best ones below.

Here is the melody of "Go Tell Aunt Rhodie" and a variation.
Using the same rhythm, make up two variations of your own.
Don't change the melody much.
Play new variations each day then write your two best examples.

Theme

Variation

Your Variation No. 1

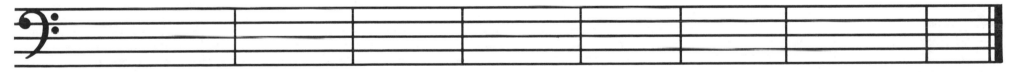

Your Variation No. 2

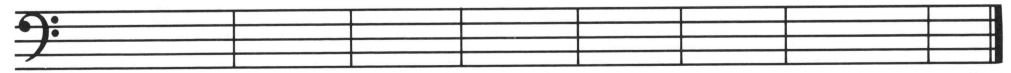

Here the pattern is repeated beginning on a higher tone.
You will recall we call this a sequence.
Make up two melodies with sequences in $\frac{2}{4}$ meter then try one in $\frac{3}{4}$.

ASSIGNED____ COMPLETED____							COMMENTS:
WEEK	M	T	W	Th	F	S	Su	
1st								
2nd								
3rd								

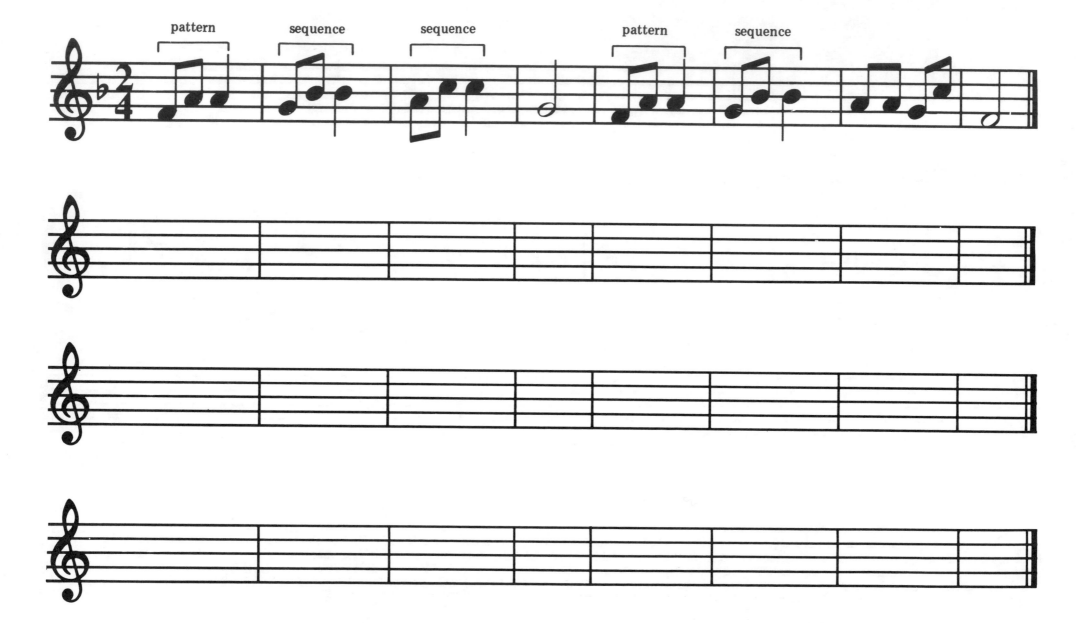

Play this theme several times, then play the variation.
Next make up several of your own and write two of
your best ones on this page.

Key of A♭ Major

ASSIGNED_____ COMPLETED_____ COMMENTS:								
WEEK	M	T	W	Th	F	S	Su	
1st								_____
2nd								_____
3rd								_____

Make these flat key signatures in treble and bass clef.

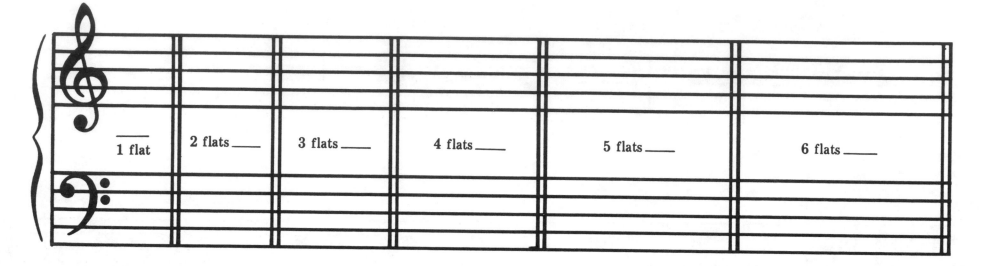

Make these sharp key signatures in treble and bass clef.

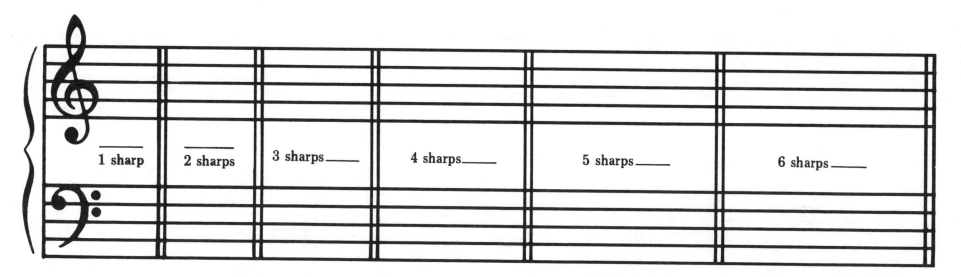

QUESTION AND ANSWER

ASSIGNED____ COMPLETED____ COMMENTS:								
WEEK	M	T	W	Th	F	S	Su	
1st								
2nd								
3rd								

The first phrase (4 bars) asks a *question*.
The second phrase gives an *answer*.

Here is another answer to the same question.

After playing many answers, write your two best ones below. Begin your answer like the question and end on G (do).

Also create your own questions, then make up new answers.

QUESTION AND ANSWER

ASSIGNED____ COMPLETED____	COMMENTS:
WEEK M T W Th F S Su	
1st	
2nd	
3rd	

If the answer begins exactly like the question (see the first measure of each) it is a *parallel answer*.

Here is another answer to the same question.

Make up other parallel answers, then write two of your favorites.

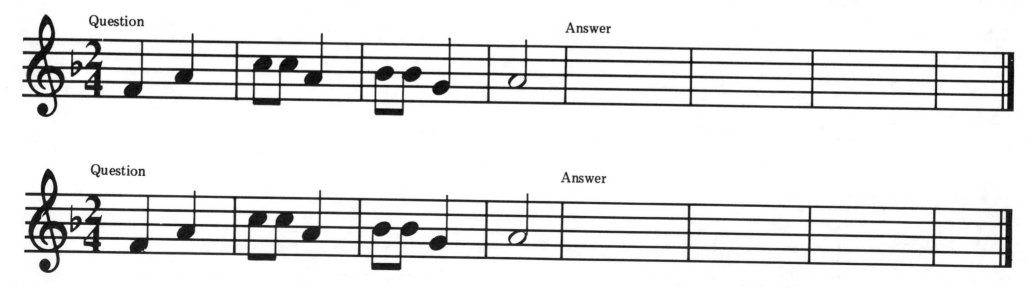

QUESTION AND ANSWER

ASSIGNED____		COMPLETED____			COMMENTS:		
WEEK	M	T	W	Th	F	S	Su
1st							
2nd							
3rd							

Remember that a *sequence* is a pattern that is repeated on different tones of the scale.
Play the question then make up answers with sequences and write the one you like best.

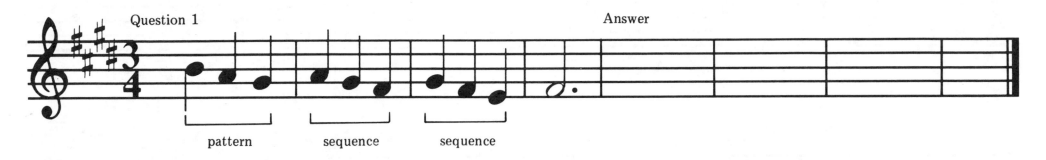

KEY SIGNATURE REVIEW

ASSIGNED____ COMPLETED____ COMMENTS:								
WEEK	M	T	W	Th	F	S	Su	_____
1st								_____
2nd								_____
3rd								_____

Fill in these major key signatures in treble and bass clef.
Also play the sharps and flats on the piano.

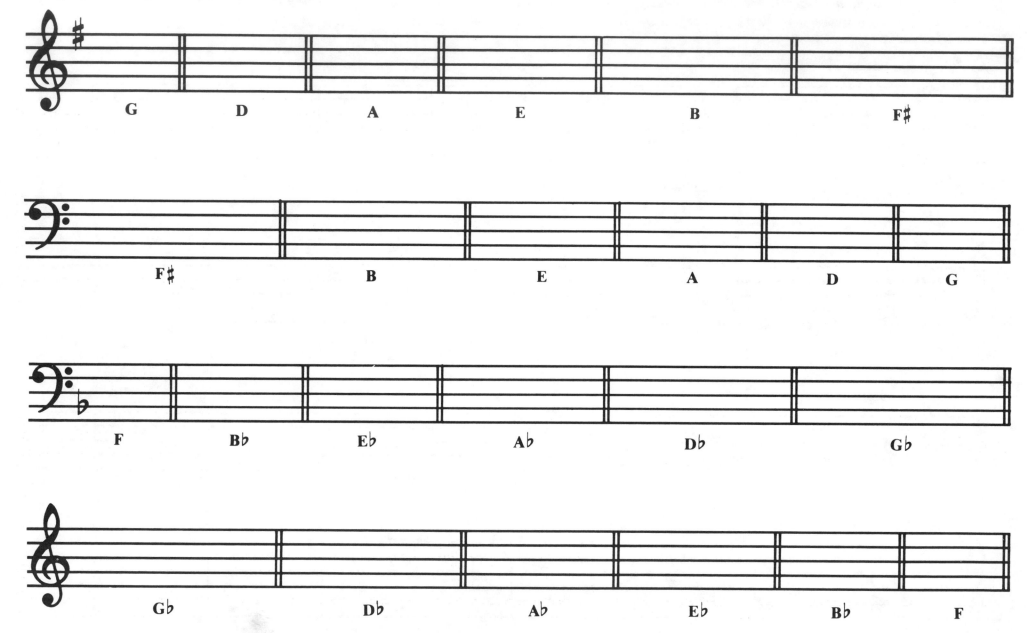

G   D   A   E   B   F#

F#   B   E   A   D   G

F   Bb   Eb   Ab   Db   Gb

Gb   Db   Ab   Eb   Bb   F

ASSIGNED____ COMPLETED____ COMMENTS:								
WEEK	M	T	W	Th	F	S	Su	
1st								
2nd								
3rd								

Set 1. The triads C, F, and G are all white keys only. Play and write them.

Set 2. The triads D, E, and A have a black key in the middle. Play and write them.

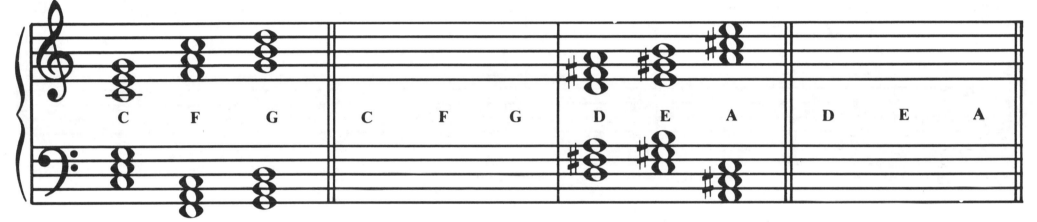

Write the triads of Set 2 (black key in the middle)

Write the triads of Set 1 (all white keys)

Write the following triads in treble and bass clef and then play each.

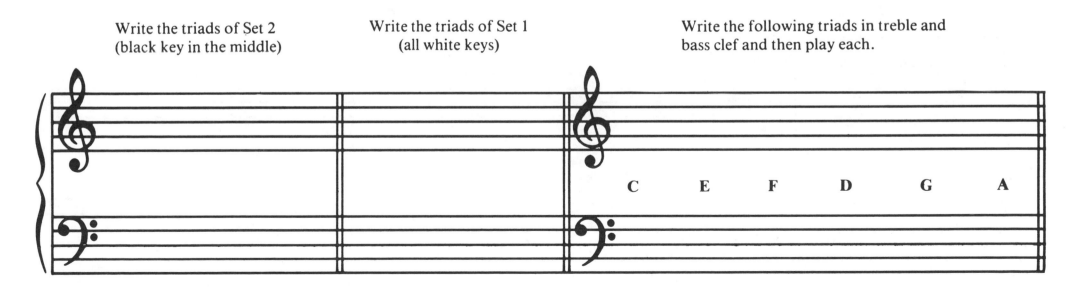

28

Finish this melody using only the tones of the G Major
chord and write the I chord in the bass of each measure.
Each day create a new chord tone melody in $\frac{2}{4}$ time.

ASSIGNED		COMPLETED				COMMENTS:	
WEEK	M	T	W	Th	F	S	Su
1st							
2nd							
3rd							

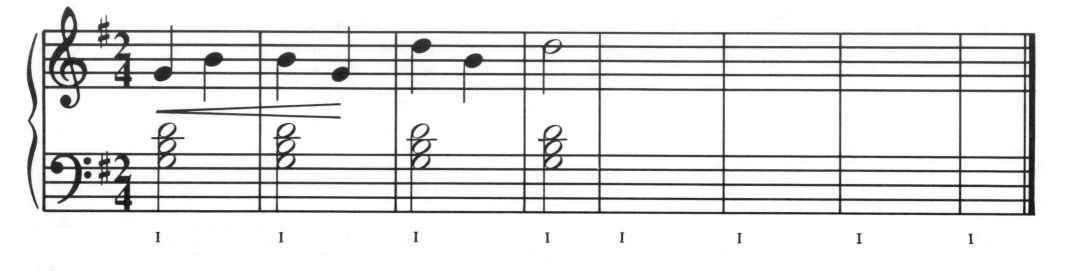

Use only the tones of the E♭ Major chord to finish this melody.
Write a I chord in the bass of each measure.
Make up other melodies for this chord.

2244

Set 3.   Db, Eb and Ab have a white key in the middle. Play and write them.

Set 4.   Gb, Bb and B are each different. Play and write them as you see how they are different.

Write the three triads from both Set 3 and Set 4.

Write the following triads in treble and bass clef then play each.

Draw the I and V₇ chords directly below the examples.
play each group of chords.

ASSIGNED____ COMPLETED____ COMMENTS:								
WEEK	M	T	W	Th	F	S	Su	
1st								____
2nd								____
3rd								____

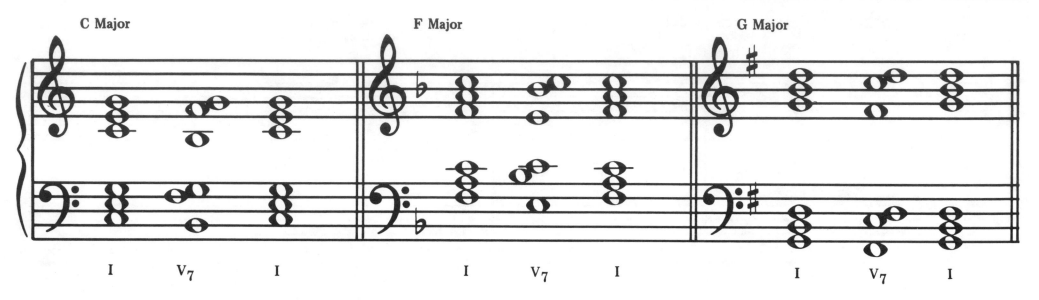

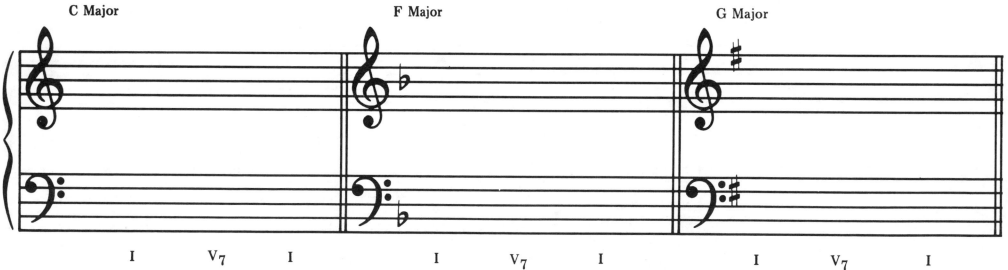

ASSIGNED_____ COMPLETED_____								COMMENTS:
WEEK	M	T	W	Th	F	S	Su	
1st								
2nd								
3rd								

Play the I, V₇ and I chords as they are written.   Draw the chords in the measures below.

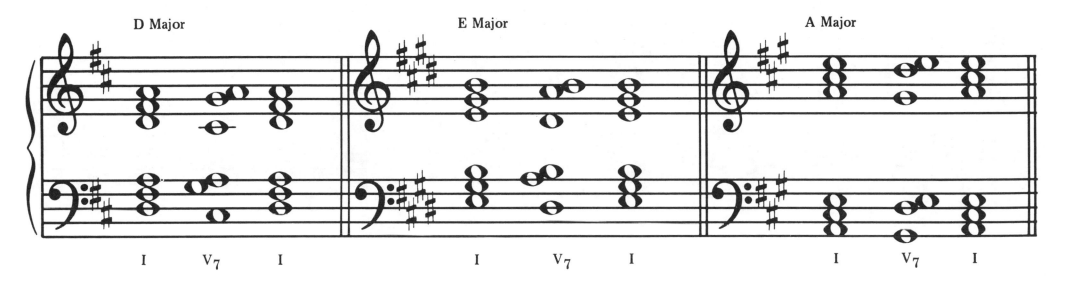

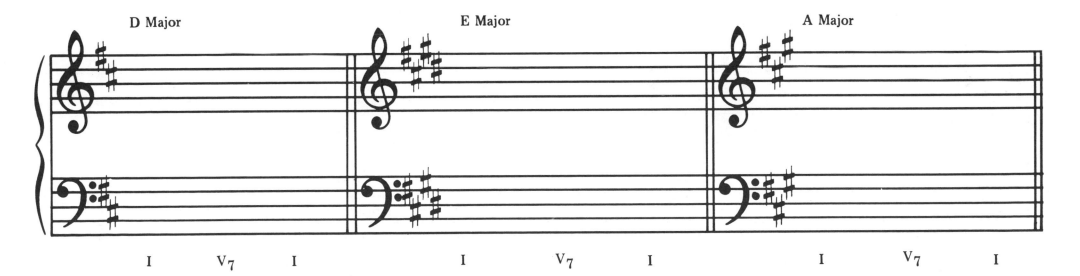

Play these chords, then draw them in the measures below.

ASSIGNED____ COMPLETED____ COMMENTS:								
WEEK	M	T	W	Th	F	S	Su	_____
1st								_____
2nd								_____
3rd								_____

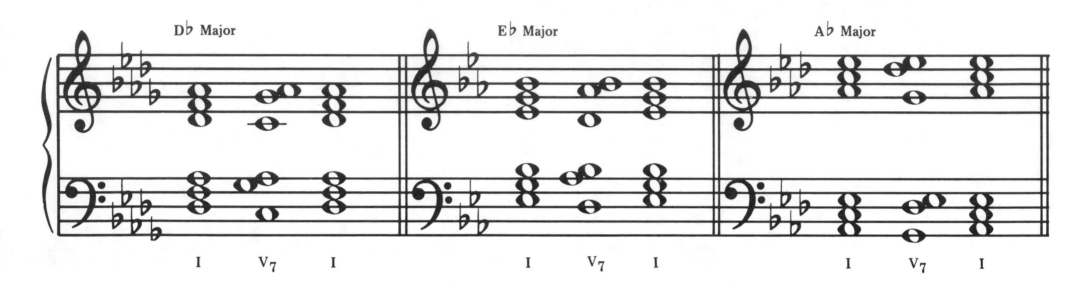

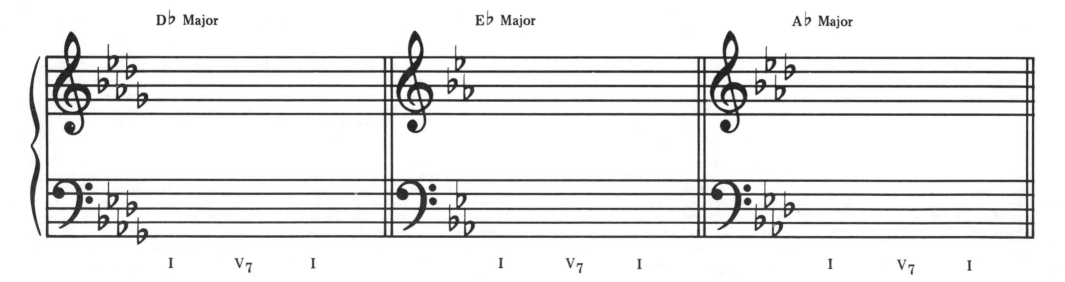

Play these chords, then draw them in the measures below.

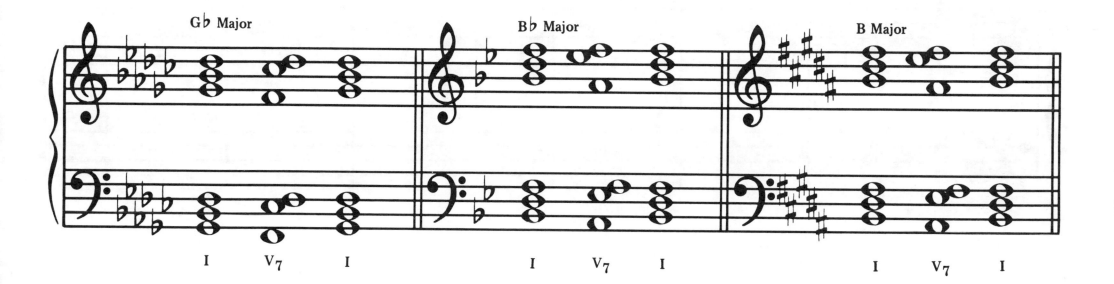

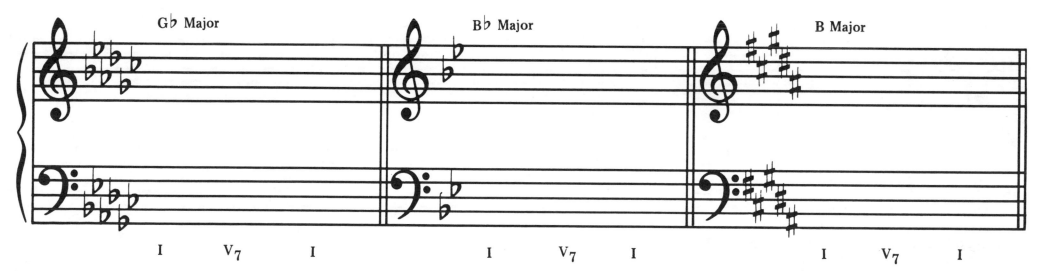

Harmonize these melodies with the I and V₇ chords.

Put the Roman numerals where they belong.

ASSIGNED____ COMPLETED____								COMMENTS:
WEEK	M	T	W	Th	F	S	Su	
1st								
2nd								
3rd								

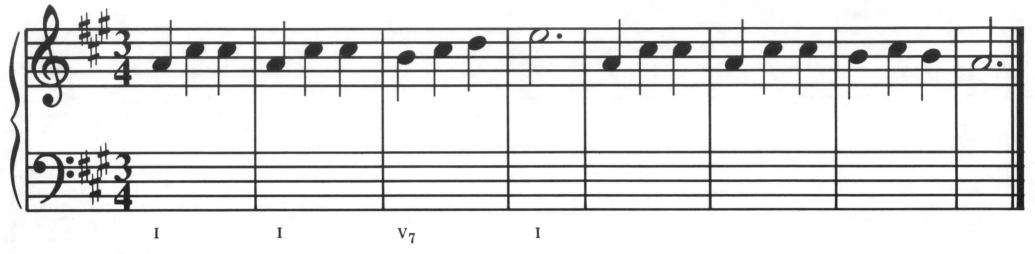

Play and transpose to the Key of G Major.

Play and transpose to the Keys of G and B Major.

ASSIGNED____ COMPLETED____								COMMENTS:
WEEK	**M**	**T**	**W**	**Th**	**F**	**S**	**Su**	
1st								
2nd								
3rd								

Put chords and their Roman numerals with these melodies. Use only I and V_7 chords.

ASSIGNED ___ COMPLETED ___ COMMENTS:								
WEEK	M	T	W	Th	F	S	Su	___
1st								___
2nd								___
3rd								___

1. Play this melody and harmonize it with I and V_7 chords "block" style.
2. Next, write the number of the chord under the bass clef.
3. Finally, write a waltz bass for the left hand (see first measure).

1. Play the melody and fill in the missing notes. Also harmonize it with block chords.
2. Write the chord numbers under the bass clef.
3. Fill in the "march bass."

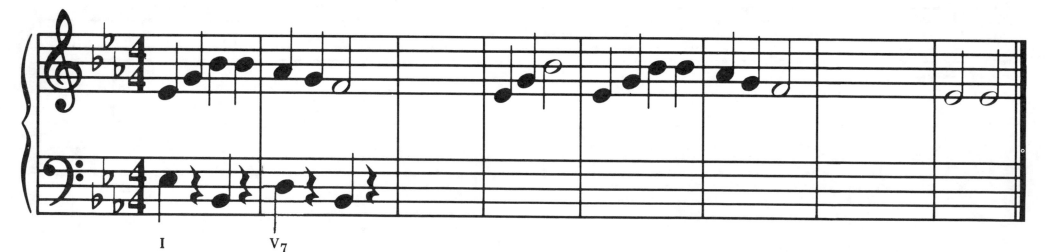

ASSIGNED____ COMPLETED____							COMMENTS:
WEEK	M	T	W	Th	F	S	Su
1st							
2nd							
3rd							

Complete these melodies then harmonize with the I and V₇ chords.
Write the chord number under each measure.
Be sure to put in expression marks (dynamics).

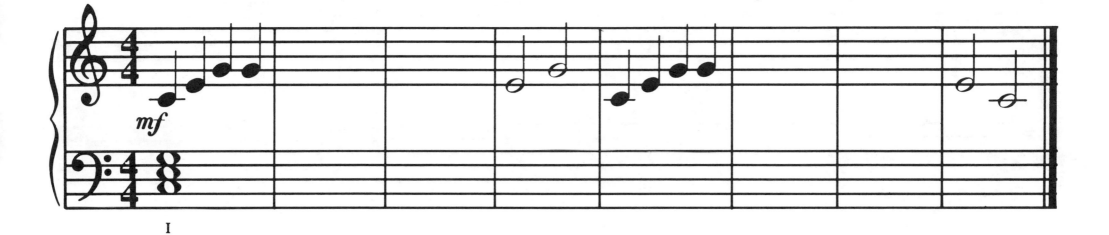

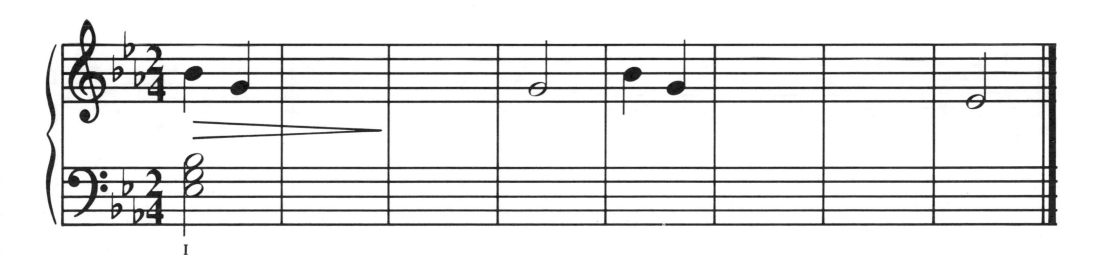

Write the I V₇ I chords then play in each key.

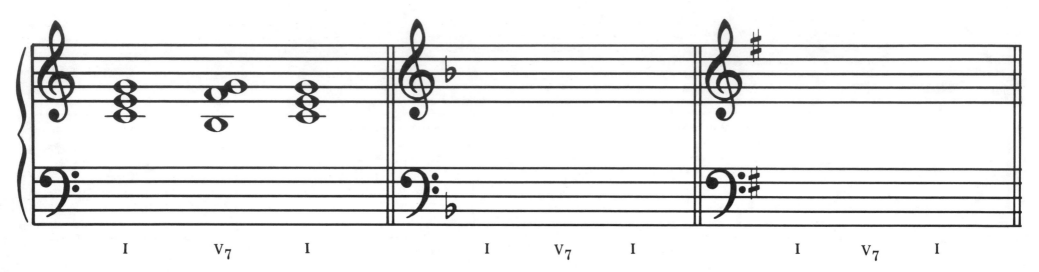

MAJOR TRIADS

Write these major triads in treble and bass clef, then play them.

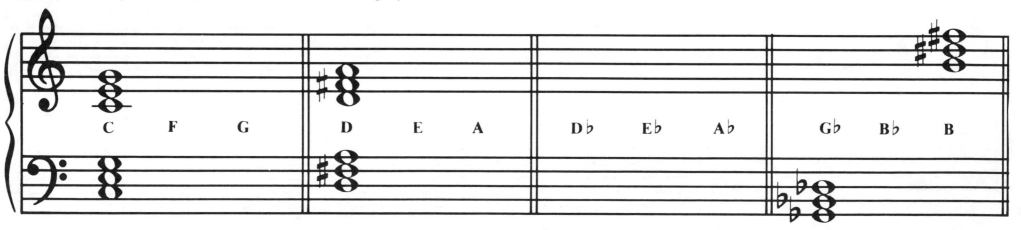

ASSIGNED____ COMPLETED____							COMMENTS:	
WEEK	M	T	W	Th	F	S	Su	_____
1st								_____
2nd								_____
3rd								_____

Write the I V₇ I chords in the blanks, then play them each day.

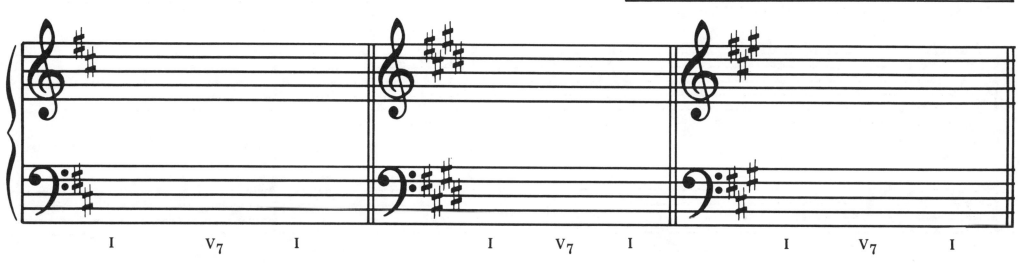

Play these questions and make up several answers with sequences. Write the ones you like the best.
Mark the sequences.

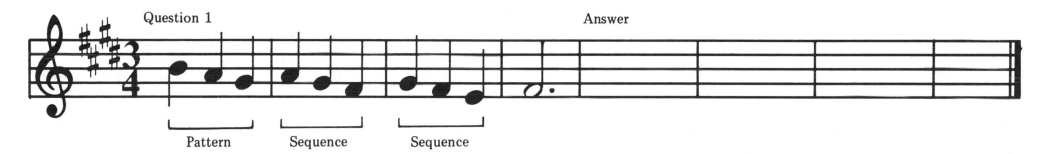

MINOR TRIADS

ASSIGNED____ COMPLETED____ COMMENTS:								
WEEK	M	T	W	Th	F	S	Su	_____
1st								_____
2nd								_____
3rd								_____

1. Write each chord first in major then in minor.

2.

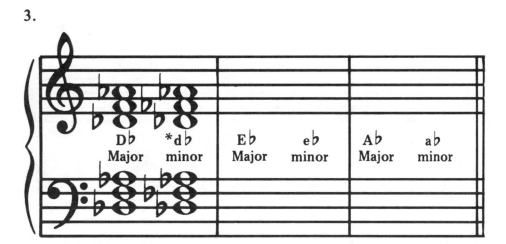

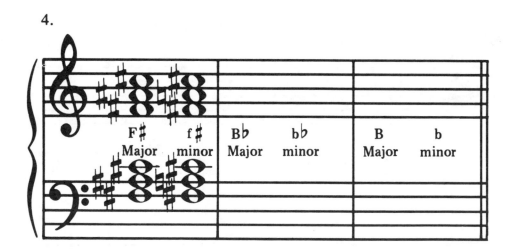

3.

4.

*usually written as c♯ minor.

ASSIGNED____ COMPLETED____ COMMENTS:							
WEEK	M	T	W	Th	F	S	Su
1st							
2nd							
3rd							

Write the minor I   V₇   I chords in the following keys.

Notice that the lowest tone of the V₇ must be raised each time by adding either a ♮ or a ♯.

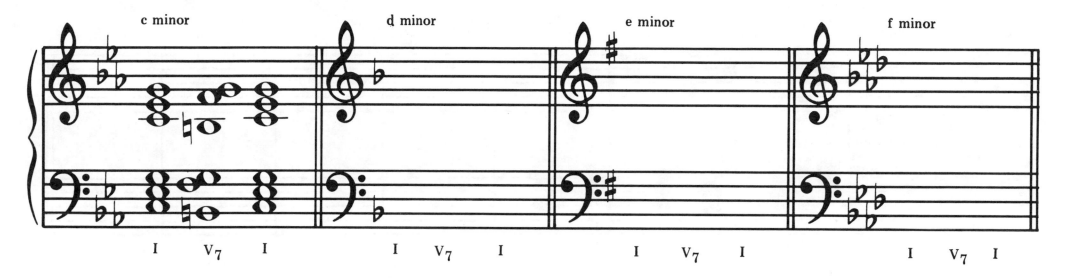

Make up parallel and contrasting answers to this question. Also fill in the chords.

After creating many answers, write one in your book.

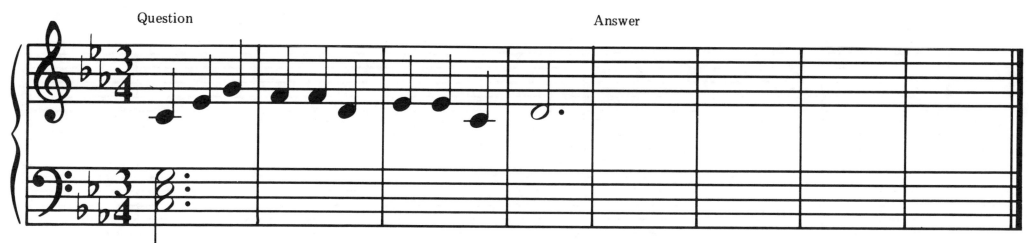

ASSIGNED____ COMPLETED____								COMMENTS:
WEEK	M	T	W	Th	F	S	Su	
1st								
2nd								
3rd								

This question is harmonized with both major and minor triads moving up and down the C Major scale.
Write the bass chords but create many answers before writing in your book.

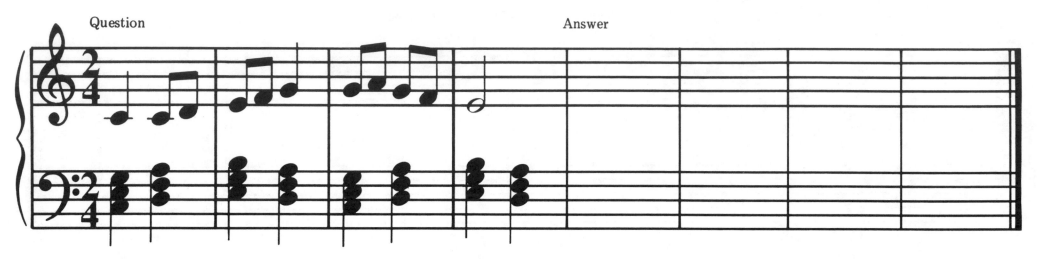

Here you can play both major and minor chords together (bichordal).
The constantly repeated pattern in the bass is called an *ostinato*.

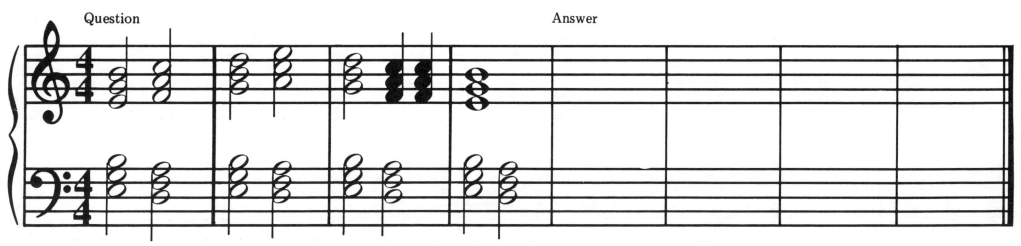

ASSIGNED____ COMPLETED____ COMMENTS:								
WEEK	M	T	W	Th	F	S	Su	
1st								
2nd								
3rd								

Make up two parallel and two contrasting answers each day for three days.
Then create a new question each day and again make up parallel and contrasting answers.

This question uses the Dorian Mode (white keys from D to D) and is harmonized by an ostinato in the left hand. After creating several answers make up other Dorian questions and answers.

This question is harmonized with an ''Alberti Bass.''
Be sure the melody is louder than the left hand accompaniment.
Use this bass pattern to create many other questions and answers.

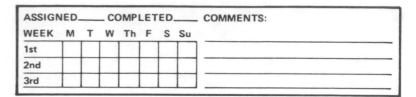

ASSIGNED____ COMPLETED____ COMMENTS:								
WEEK	M	T	W	Th	F	S	Su	
1st								
2nd								
3rd								

Write the following major and minor triads.

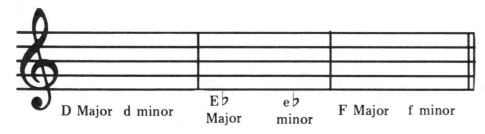

D Major   d minor   E♭ Major   e♭ minor   F Major   f minor

Write the key signature and I   V₇   I chords for D♭ and E Major.

D♭ Major   E Major
I   V₇   I   I   V₇   I

2244

Find the sequence and inversion in the question then use these ideas in your answer.
Harmonize this with a waltz style bass and mark the chord numbers.
Make up new questions with sequences, repetitions and inversions.

Write and play these major triads.

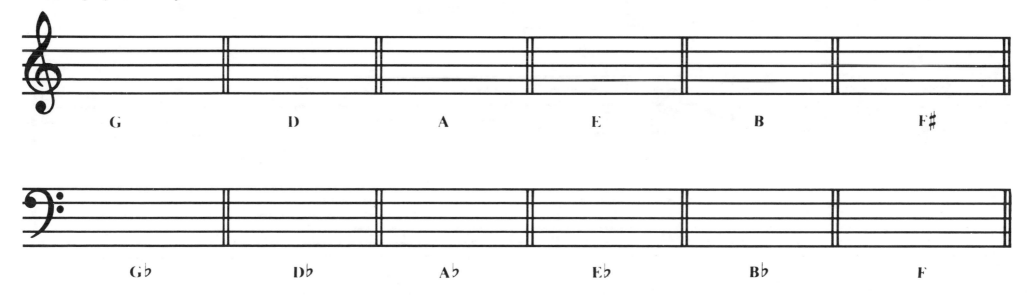

G   D   A   E   B   F♯

G♭   D♭   A♭   E♭   B♭   F

ASSIGNED____ COMPLETED____								COMMENTS:
WEEK	M	T	W	Th	F	S	Su	____
1st								____
2nd								____
3rd								____

This question is harmonized with triads moving up and down the D Major scale.
Use this ostinato to harmonize your answers.

Here triads in both hands move up and down the white keys between D and D (Dorian scale).
Use this idea to compose a piece of your own built on triads in both hands.

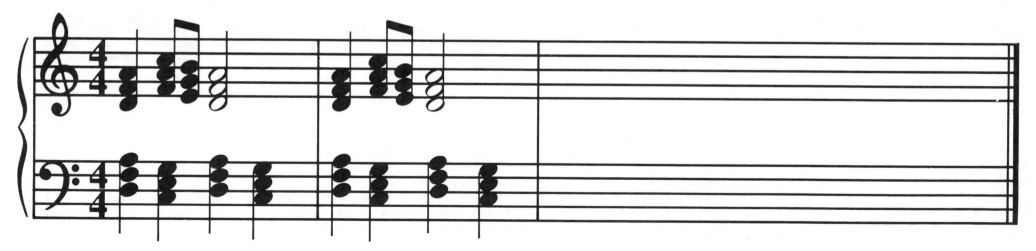

ASSIGNED____ COMPLETED____	COMMENTS:						
WEEK	M	T	W	Th	F	S	Su
1st							
2nd							
3rd							

Here are some of the bass patterns you have used in this book.
Try them with the questions on this page, then create questions of your own.

Block Chord   Broken Chord   Waltz Bass   March Bass   Alberti Bass

Question   Answer

Question   Answer

Question   Answer

2244

ASSIGNED____ COMPLETED____ COMMENTS:							
WEEK	M	T	W	Th	F	S	Su
1st							
2nd							
3rd							

Write the following major key signatures
in treble and bass.

D Major   B Major   A♭ Major

Make the following triads.

F♯ Major   f♯ minor   A Major   a minor   B♭ Major   b♭ minor

Write the following minor key signatures
in treble and bass.

c minor   b minor   g minor

Write the key signature and I V₇ I chords for
D Major and d minor.

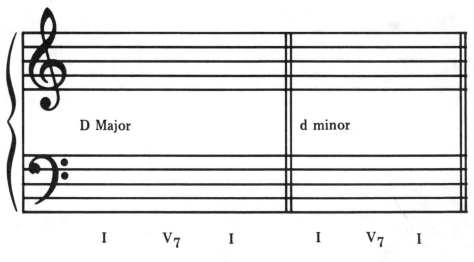

D Major   d minor

I   V₇   I   I   V₇   I